Table of Contents

Legal Notes and Disclaimer

Legal & Disclaimer

The information contained in this book and its contents is not designed to replace or take the place of any form of medical or professional advice; and is not meant to replace the need for independent medical, financial, legal or other professional advice or services, as may be required. The content and information in this book havebeen provided for educational and entertainment purposes only.

The content and information contained in this book havebeen compiled from sources deemed reliable, and it is accurate to the best of the Author's knowledge, information, and belief. However, the Author cannot guarantee its accuracy and validity and cannot be held liable for any errors and omissions. Furthermore, changes can be periodically made to this book as and when needed. Where appropriate and necessary, you must consult a professionalbefore using any of the suggested remedies, techniques, or information in this book.

Upon using the contents and information contained in this book, you agree to hold harmless the Author from and against any damages, costs, and expenses, including any legal fees potentially resulting from the application of any of the information provided by this book. This disclaimer applies to any loss, damages or injury caused by the use and application, whether directly or indirectly, of any advice or information presented, whether for breach of contract, tort, negligence, personal injury, criminal intent, or under any other cause of action.

You agree to accept all risks of using the information presented inside this book.

You agree that by continuing to read this book, where appropriate and/or necessary, you shall consult a professional before using any of the suggested remedies, techniques, or information in this book.

CHAPTER 1. SO, WHAT IS MS EXCEL SHORTCUTS

In short Excel, shortcuts are the keyboard combinations that can guide excel to perform aparticular action (task) with the use of a pointing device or simply the mouse.

For an occasional user, this might not be of much interest but for people who use it for – say 50% of the time when they are in their offices this is going to be a great time saver.

So in this book, we are going to explore the shortcut keys in context of the various features of Excel and the things we usually do with them. The benefit we will get is twofold:

- We will learn a shortcut key
- We will also get arevision of an important feature of Excel.

A little bit of theory – a note on Muscle Memory

The Wikipedia describes muscle memory[1] as:

"The ability to reproduce a particular movement without conscious thought acquired as a result of frequent repetition of that movement."

The definition is self-explanatory – in our daily life, we repeat acertain task that makes your body learn how to perform that task without having to plan it – it is done automatically to some extent.

Muscle Memory and Keyboard Shortcuts

- How often we have to do "copy" and "paste" function.
- How often we do insert rows or add a pivot table to our workbook?
- How frequently we have to shuffle between workbooks or worksheets?

These questions and many similar others can be answered by taking into account the muscle memory our bodies can build and the keyboard shortcut we are going to discuss in the following pages.

The development of muscle memory relies on the something called "motor nerves" that can be made to learn the steps to perform these tasks. This collectively builds our muscle memory. An example of muscle memory is when a person driving the cars for the first time finds it difficult to synch its body to change gears, press brake and clutch simultaneously. Once he is done with this muscle memory development phase, he does so unintentionally – without any significant planned effort.

The Ergonomic aspect of keyboard shortcuts

The ergonomic mode of keyboard use can lead to reduced stress in hand (while using thekeyboard) and more result in increased productivity[2] hence if you want "healthy hands" do use keyboard shortcuts.

The two modes of Excel Shortcut keys

There are two types of excel shortcut keys:

- Conventional shortcuts – one that requires theuse of Alt, Ctrl, Shift along with the use of alphabets, numerals and function keys.

---

[1] https://en.wikipedia.org/wiki/Muscle_memory
[2] https://ehs.ucsf.edu/ergonomic-keyboard-shortcuts

Quick Access Toolbar shorts – this type of shortcut provided through the Quick Access Toolbars. The shortcuts are invoked by pressing Alt Key and then keying in the sequence of alphabets will execute the desired command.

In this booklet, we are going to cover both of these types of shortcuts.

Moving ahead with Keyboard shortcuts

The first and the foremost operation when using excel is to open a workbook. After opening we might:

- Type in data or append more data
- Format it
- Convert it to table
- Add subtotals
- Otherwise, insert a pivot table
- Put in a formula
- Conditional format a formula

And so on. We will take these possibilities one by one and see shortcuts for them.

CHAPTER 2. WORKING WITH WORKBOOK AND WORKSHEETS

The workbook is the founding stone of whatever we want to do in MS Excel. Let's assume that you have to prepare a report for aparticular purpose. You want to have a blank new sheet to start with. Once you have opened the MS excel window, you can open the new workbook by pressing certain key combinations.

In the following examples, we are exploring the use of keys commonly used for creating new workbooks, adding new worksheets and saving and closing them.

Example Task # 01

Opening a Work Book, add a new worksheet, key in some text and save the file

To achieve this task with keyboard shortcut keys, use following shortcut keys:

Solution:

Open a New Works	Ctrl + N
Navigate to the second sheet	Ctrl + Page Down
Keys in some Text	Use Keyboard to type
Save the File	Ctrl + S and Name the file

Example Task # 02

Dock down the current file, open a new file add some data, go to the previous worksheet and save changes to both of the files

Minimize Current Workbook	Ctrl + F9
Open a New Works	Ctrl + N
Go to the last Workbook	Ctrl + Shift + Tab
Keys in some Text	Use Keyboard to type
Save the File	Ctrl + S
Toggle to new workbook	Ctrl + Shift
Save the File	Ctrl + S and Name the file

Example Task # 03

You are done with the editing function, print both of the files, save changes once again, and close both of the workbooks and the Excel window.

Print the current file	Ctrl + P
Save the current file	Ctrl + S
Close the current file	Ctrl + F4

Print the second file	Ctrl + P
Save changes to the file	Ctrl + S
Close the second file	Ctrl + F4
Close the Excel Window	Alt + F4

Understanding the Tool Tip Sequence for Shortcut keys

The tooltipsequence is a new feature stat started from Excel 2010 and is a handy way of accessing features in excel. The feature is activated by pressing Alt Key first and then following the desired sequence as they tooltipsappear in the form of alphabets on various features.

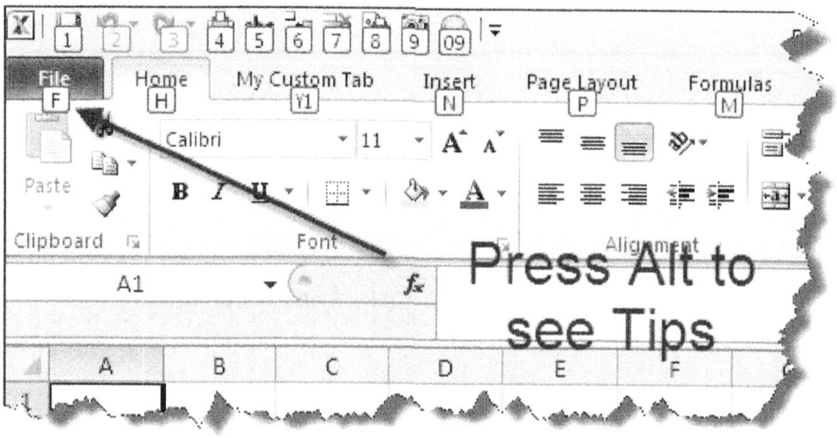

The same task that we were performing with these key sequence for example:

To Open the New workbook	– Press Alt F N N
To Open the Open File dialogue box	– Press Alt F O
To Save Changes to Current File	– Press Alt F S
To Save a workbook as new File	– Press Alt F A

You just need to follow the Tipsvisually, and it will act a keyboard shortcut.

The Keys (Used) in this Chapter

S.No	**Shortcut Key**	**Purpose**
	Open Workbook	Ctrl + N
	Access “Open File” Dialogue Box	Ctrl + O
	Add a New Worksheet	Shift + F11
	Save Current File	Ctrl + S
	Print File	Ctrl + P
	Save File As Dialogue Box	F12
	Close Active Workbook	Ctrl+F4
	Close Excel Window	Alt+F4
	Toggle Tab	Alt + Left / Right Keys

S.No	Shortcut Key	Purpose
	To insert a new worksheet	Shift + F11
	Navigate to next worksheet	Ctrl + Page Down Key
	Navigate to the previous sheet	Ctrl + Page UP Key
	Go to next workbook	Ctrl + Tab
	Go to the previous workbook	Ctrl + Shift + Tab
	Minimize current workbook	Ctrl + F9
	Maximize current workbook	Ctrl + F10

CHAPTER 3. BASIC OPERATION ON WORKSHEETS AND CELLS

We use aspreadsheet to add manage out data, so simply opening and saving a file should not be the only thing we usually do. Infect whenever we save a workbook, it is often preceded by some "changes" that we into that workbook.

The list of basic operations is exhaustive, but just to mention few that are most frequently done include:

- Copy - Paste or cut – paste data
- Inserting or deleting cells
- Using paste special dialogue box
- Performing search with find and replacing with Replace
- Inserting charts etc

Here are some scenarios where you can use these keys to improve productivity.

Example Task # 04

You want to quickly copy and paste data to another sheet but only values without any formatting or formulas:

Copy the data	Ctrl + C
[Select the cell to paste]	
Access paste-special menu	Ctrl + Alt + V
Use Tab button to select "value" to paste only value	

Alternatively, you can access the same thing with Tool Tips by following these keys:

Copy the data	Alt H C > Enter
Access paste-special menu	Alt H V S >Enter

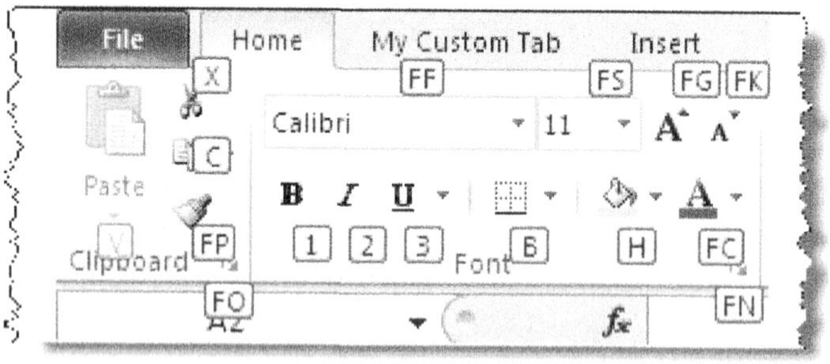

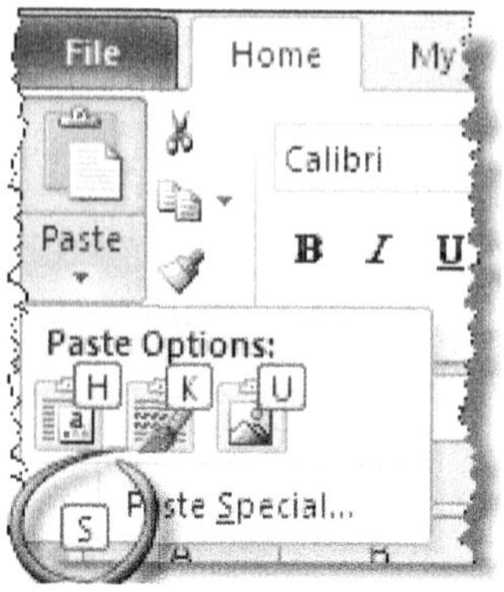

Example Task # 05

You have wanted to convert a range to an excel table and disable filters in the table:

Convert Current Range to Table	Ctrl + T
Insert a chart as object in sheet	Ctrl + Shift + L

The same thing can be done through **Alt H T** and Entering Press twice. Similarly, we can insert a chart **Alt N C** (if you want to add a column chart) or choose an option you want.

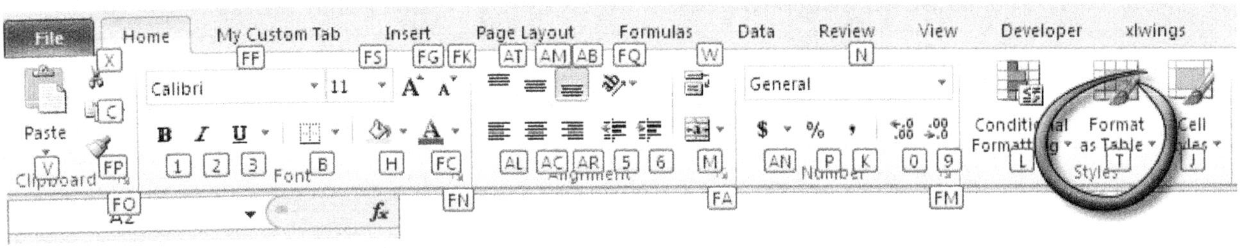

The Keys (Used) in this Chapter

S.No	Shortcut Key	Purpose
	Cut a Cell's Contents	Ctrl + X
	Paste a Cell's Contents	Ctrl + V
	Copy cell's contents	Ctrl + C
	Cut and Insert between two cells	Shift & Drag to the cell
	Copy and Insert between two cells	Ctrl + Shift & Drag to the cell
	Undo thelast action	Ctrl + Z
	Display Paste Special Dialogue Box	Ctrl + Alt + V
	Redo last action	Ctrl + Y
	To repeat the last command/action	Press F4
	Accessing Find Dialogue Box	Ctrl + F
	Accessing Replace Dialogue Box	Ctrl + H
	To find last match	Ctrl + Shift + F4
	To find the next match	Shift + F4
	Insert a Chart in a Sheet	Alt + F1
	Insert chart as a new sheet	F11
	Insert or Enable Filter	Ctrl + Shift + L
	Activate Filter Options	Alt + Down Key
	Convert Range to a table	Ctrl + T
	To select row of a table	Shift + Spacebar
	To Select column of a table	Ctrl + Space
	Select an entire Table	Ctrl + A

CHAPTER 4. MOVING AROUND– WORKSHEETS, ROWS, COLUMNS, AND CELLS

As we go entering data into a sheet, we continue from this point to that in the sheet. Often the moment is time-consuming as we have to switch between the pointer device and the keyboard. To overcome this hurdle, we can use keyboard shortcuts that are reeled to navigation or are meant for working around in the sheet.

The table that follows these lines list most of the keyboard shortcuts that are there to be used in such case. But as we have been doing, we will follow the examples first:

Example Task # 05

You want to delete an entire row quickly!

Select the entire row	Shift + Space
Delete	Press Delete

Example Task # 06

The table you are working with contains some blank column, and you want to quickly move the next column with data (and skip all empty columns) and then back to the starting column.

From the current cell	Alt + Right Arrow
From the (now) current cell	Alt + Left Arrow

Example Task # 06

You are somewhere on the sheet; you want to get to the starting point.

To go to the first cell	Press Ctrl + Home

Now we might want to do it with tooltips, but it should be noted that with toll tips we can only access options that are present in the MS Excel ribbon. Hence we will stick to these shortcuts only for this case.

The Keys (Used) in this Chapter

S.No	Shortcut Key	Purpose
	Selecting an entire row	Shift + Space
	Selecting an entire column	Ctrl + Space
	Move right to next non-empty cell	Ctrl + Right Arrow
	Move left to next non-empty cell	Ctrl + Left Arrow
	Move the screen to right – one complete screen	Alt + Page Down
	Move the screen to left – one complete screen	Alt + Page Up
	Move the screen Down – one complete screen	Page Down
	Move the screen Up – one complete screen	Page Up
	Go to the right or left side of Data Region	Ctrl + Right/Left Arrow
	Go to the top or bottom side of Data Region	Ctrl + Up/Down Arrow
	Move to the first cell – (leftmost cell) in row	Press Home Button
	Move to cell A1	Ctrl + Home

Chapter 5. Shortcut Keys to Select Ranges

When you want to apply formatting to some cells, we select them by holding Ctrl key and pointing our cursor to the cell where towant to selecttoo. But when we do this action repeatedly it becomes boredom or perhaps a task that irritates us a lot.

In this part, we will discuss keys that can be used to select ranges quickly – whatever be the purpose.

Example Task # 07

You want to select a range quickly. How will you do it?

While thefirst cell being selected	
Press Keys	Ctrl + Shift
Point to direction – downward select	Press Down Key
Rightward select	Press Right Key

..As usually we move from top to bottom and left to right in a spreadsheet, this will select the entire table that you want to format.

Example Task # 09

You want to select a row till last available data entry. How will you do it?

While thefirst cell being selected	
Press Keys	Ctrl + Shift
Rightward select	Press Right Key

In this way, you can be quicker while selecting the ranges.

The Keys (Used) in this Chapter

S.No	Shortcut Key	Purpose
	Cover selection to one cell on the right or left side	Shift + Right/Left Arrow
	Cover Selection to one cell on the top or bottom	Shift + Top/bottom Arrow
	Select till last cell to left or right	Ctrl + Shift + Left/Right Arrow
	Select till last cell to up or down	Ctrl + Shift + Up/Down Arrow
	Select from current cell to first cell (A1)	Ctrl + Shift + Home
	Selecting an entire screen –leftward	Alt + Shift + Page Up
	Selecting an entire screen-rightward	Alt + Shift + Page Down
	Selecting an entire screen upward	Shift + Page Up
	Selecting an entire screen downward	Shift + Page Down

CHAPTER 6. ACCESSING OPTIONS IN "GOTO-SPECIAL" DIALOGUE BOX AND FORMULA AUDITING

There is avariety of types of cells present in a spreadsheet. They could be formulas, constants, comments,etc. that make up a sheet. Most of these options are available through GoTo Special dialogue box, and it could be accessed by pressing anF5 key or by pressing Ctrl+G.

In the following example will see how to use shortcuts to access this dialogue box.

Example Task # 10

You want to select only cells that have the formulato format them for color. How will you select cells with formulas only?

Select the region	Ctrl + Shift + Right + Down
	Arrow key
Access the Go To Dialogue box	Press F5 (or Ctrl + G)
Reach Go To Special Dialogue box	Press Tab Twice
Select cell that has formula only	Use Tab to select option

Example Task # 11

You have successfully selected the cells with formula only; now you want to select only those cells that have errors. How will you do it?

After reaching the option to select
Press double tab to arrive at the Go To special dialogue box
Use tab to select the formula
Use tab further to unselect everything except "Errors."

The Keys (Used) in this Chapter

S.No	Shortcut Key	Purpose
	Display "Go To" Dialogue Box	Ctrl + G or Press F5
	To select cell containing "Comments"	Ctrl + Shift + O
	To select region of adjacent cells[3]	Ctrl + Shift + * or Ctrl + A
	To select all cells – direct precedents for a cell	Ctrl + [
	To select all cells – direct dependents for a cell	Ctrl +]
	To select all cells – direct & indirect precedents	Ctrl + Shift + {
	To select all cells – direct & indirect dependents	Ctrl + Shift + }

[3] Press asterisk from QWERTY keyboard and not from numeric pad.

CHAPTER 7. SHORTCUT KEYS FOR DATA ENTRY

For repeated tasks that require speed and accuracy, following keys are essential to practice. The keys are self-explanatory, but following hints are helpful when using them

Example Task # 12

I am entering data across row, from left to right, but suddenly entered a wrong entry, how can I move back to thelast cell on the left?

Move left	Press Shift + Tab

Example Task # 13

I am entering data in thecolumn, from top to bottom, but suddenly entered a wrong entry, how can I move back to thelast cell upward?

Move left	Press Shift + Enter

Important Points to be noted:

- If pressing enter move it one cell down, shift-enter will make it move one cell up.
- If pressing tab tomove it one cell to theright, shift and tab will make it move one cell left.
- If you want to calculate a formula and still want to stay in the same cell, use ctrl and enter.

The Keys (Used) in this Chapter

S.No	Shortcut Key	Purpose
	Moving one cell down after editing[4]	Press Enter
	Moving one cell up after editing	Press Shift + Enter
	Moving one cell to right	Press Tab
	Moving one cell to left	Press Shift + Tab
	To stay in a cell after pressing Enter	Ctrl + Enter
	To enter same data in more than one selected cells	Ctrl + Enter
	To insert current date	Ctrl + ;
	To insert current time	Ctrl + Shift + ;
	Copy Data from cell to the right side	Ctrl + R
	Copy Data from cell from above	Ctrl + D

[4] It depends on how you have setup the movement of Enter Key – If you have custom set the active cell to move right ward (or any other direction), pressing enter will move in that direction and shift + enter in opposite direction. The default setting is when active cell is moving down wards when pressed Enter.

CHAPTER 8. CELLS

MANAGING CELL EDITS

When we want to edit an excel cell, we press F2 keys. After pressing F2 and bringing cell in edit mode, we delete, add cell contents or select it to make some changes. In the following section of shortcut keys, we will explore options to select contents of thecell.

Example Task # 13

I am entering data in thecolumn, from top to bottom, but suddenly entered a wrong entry, how can I move back to thelast cell upward?

Move left	Press Shift + Enter

Example Task # 14

I have entered thewrong first name of mine, what is the way I can delete just my first name?

Enable edit mode	Press F2
Move to the start of cell (left side0	Ctrl + Home
Select the first word (first name)	Ctrl + Shift + right arrow
Delete the word	Press Delete

The Keys (Used) in this Chapter

S.No	Shortcut Key	Purpose
	Edit contents of the active cell	Press F2
	Edit or add a comment	Shift + F2
	Selecting a cell's content in edit mode	Shift + Right / Left Arrow
	Move cursor to one word around	Ctrl + Right / Left Arrow
	Select one word around	Ctrl + Shift+ Right / Left Arrow
	Select entire cell contents in edit mode till start	Shift + Home
	Select entire cell contents in edit mode till end	Shift + End
	Select from a point till end of cell's content	Ctrl + Delete
	Delete cell's content in Edit Mode	Press Delete
	Insert a new line within cell	Alt + Enter
	Move to Start of the cell	Ctrl + Home

FORMATTING CELL

To make data presentable, we need to format it. Sometimes it is aesthetics that make us format data; on the others, it is the need to differentiate something using formatting.

Formatting cell options include manipulating options available with font and font colors, cell alignments, indentation of cells and others. We will see how we can add

Example Task # 14

Format cell contents to be bold, italic and underlined.

Make contents bold	Ctrl + B
Make contents italic	Ctrl + I
Make contents underlined	Ctrl +U

Example Task # 14

Insert an indent to cell content and increase its font size.

Increase Indent	Alt H 6
Increase font size	Alt H F G

The Keys (Used) in this Chapter

S.No	Shortcut Key	Purpose
	Bold format cell contents	Ctrl + B
	Italic format cell contents	Ctrl + I
	Underline format cell contents	Ctrl + U
	Turn on Strikethrough for a cell	Ctrl + 5
	To align cell contents to center	Alt + H + A + C
	To align cell contents to left	Alt + H + A + L
	To align cell contents to right	Alt + H + A + R
	Insert an Indent	Alt + H + 6
	Revert an Indent	Alt + H + 5
	To Increase font size	Alt + H + F + G
	To Decrease font size	Alt + H + F + K
	To change the color of font in a cell	Alt + H + FC
	To change the color of font from color template	Alt + H + F C + M
	To align cell contents to top	Alt + H + A + T
	To align cell contents to center	Alt + H + A + C
	To align cell contents to bottom	Alt + H + A + B
	To align cell contents at a counter clockwise angle	Alt + H + FQ + O
	To align cell contents at a clockwise angle	Alt + H + FQ + L
	To align cell contents at vertical angle	Alt + H + FQ + V
	To align cell contents up or down	Alt + H + FQ + U or D

HANDLING NUMBER FORMATTING

If you are working in accounts for thefinance department, you must have come across the need to format numbers in currency, in percentage or with comma separation. All these number formattings can be accessed through the Home menu, but this could also be done with shortcut keys.

In thefollowingexample,w will see how to format numbers differently:

Example Task # 14

Format a number as date

Format selected cell as date	Ctrl + Shift + #

Example Task # 14

Format a number as currency

Format selected cell as date	Ctrl + Shift + $

The Keys (Used) in this Chapter

S.No	Shortcut Key	Purpose
	Format a number as general	Ctrl + Shift + ~
	Format a number as currency	Ctrl + Shift + $
	Format a number as percentage	Ctrl + Shift + %
	Format a number in scientific mode	Ctrl + Shift + ^
	Format a number as date	Ctrl + Shift + #
	Format a number as time	Ctrl + Shift + @
	Convert to number format	Ctrl + Shift + !

FORMATTING CELLS FOR BORDERS

Usually, we border to mark a particular region. Most of the time it is a table or we separate two portions of a worksheet by drawing borders. On the other, if we want to highlight theindividual cell or a cell represents some significant result in a calculation we use theborder to highlight them.

The following shortcuts make use of the tooltipbeside the one that adds outline border to a cell. Let's understand them using few examples:

Example Task # 15

You have produced a balance sheet and now want to highlight theparticular cell with top bottom border. How will you do it with keyboard shortcuts?

Select the cell that you want to border	
For top border	Alt + H + B + P
For bottom border	Alt + H + B + O

Example Task # 16

To a great worksheet having some financial calculation, you want to highlight a cell will full thick border. How will you put aborder around the cell?

Select the cell	
For thick out side border	Alt + H + B + T

The Keys (Used) in this Chapter

S.No	Shortcut Key	Purpose
	To add outline border	Ctrl + Shift + &
	To add (or remove) right/left border	Alt + H + B + R or L
	To add (or remove) top/bottom border	Alt + H + B + P or O
	To add outside border thick	Alt + H + B + T
	To add outside border regular / thin	Alt + H + B + S
	To remove border	Alt + H + B + N
	To have all borders	Alt + H + B + A

WORKING WITH FORMULAS

Formulas are the most critical parts of a worksheet and are most prone to errors. Since they are frequently inserted, knowing their shortcuts can improve the productivity a lot. Here are few situations that might need the use of shortcuts keys followed by the detailed table:

Example Task # 17

You won't put the sum of column quickly in a cell. What will you do?

Select the cell	
To sum the cells or current region	Alt + =

Example Task # 18

You want to enter a formula as an array formula.

Select the cell	
Execute formula as an array one	Ctrl + Shift + Enter

Example Task # 19

You have a large workbook with multiple sheets, but you just want to calculate the one you are currently working on:

To calculate only current sheet	Shift + F9

Example Task # 20

You have been trying to use a function, but you barely remembered the first few characters of it, how will you complete it?

To autocomplete the function name	Press Tab as you write it

Example Task # 21

You don't want to use your pointing device for going to formula menu. Which shortcut key will you use?

Access formula dialogue box	Shift + F3

The Keys (Used) in this Chapter

S.No	Shortcut Key	Purpose
	To Open Function Dialogue Box	Shift + F3
	To sum the current region in a column	Alt + =
	To switch on / off display formula in a cell	Ctrl + `
	Enter formula as an Array formula	Ctrl + Shift + Enter
	To calculate all worksheet	F9
	To calculate only current worksheet	Shift + F9
	To force calculate all sheets	Ctrl + Shift + F9
	Expand or collapse formula bar	Ctrl + Shift + U
	Access name manager dialogue box	Ctrl + F3

	Access create name from selection dialogue box	Ctrl + Shift + F3
	Autocomplete function name	Tab

MANIPULATING SHEET'S GRIDLINES

The sheet consists of rows and columns that are identified by the row labels and column labels and the grid lines. These grid lines help read the data and can be turned on and off. These grid lines can also be formatted for colors.

The columns and rows can be grouped and ungrouped, and we can retain a row or column as well as delete it. To insert or delete the column row, you have to select it from theheader but it can also be done with keyboard shortcuts. Similarly, when selected this way, they can be hidden or unhidden, and we can do it with keyboard shortcuts.

Let's take up few examples first.

Example Task # 22

You just found that you have missed entering a complete line of record you have to insert it between two records. How will you proceed?

Select the current row	Shift + Spacebar
Insert the row	Ctrl + Shift + +

Example Task # 23

You want to insert a column between two columns. What is the shortcut key for this?

Select the current column	Ctrl + Spacebar
Insert the column	Ctrl + Shift + +

So basically to insert a column or row, we need to press **Ctrl + shift + +,**and we have to use Shift or Ctrl with spacebar to select the row or column respectively.

Example Task # 24

You came across a situation where you don't want to delete a row or column; rather you want o tohide it. How will you do it?

Select the current column	Ctrl + Spacebar
Hide column	Ctrl + 0
Select the current row	Shift + Spacebar
Hide row	Ctrl + 9

Example Task # 25

You want to group 4 columns.

Select the columns	Shift + right arrow
Show group dialogue box	Alt + Shift + Right arrow

Select the option to hide column

Press ok

The Keys (Used) in this Chapter

S.No	Shortcut Key	Purpose
	To access "insert row and column" dialogue box	Ctrl + Shift + +
	To access "display delete dialogue box"	Ctrl + -
	Select a row	Shift + spacebar
	Select a column	Ctrl + space bar
	Delete selected row	Ctrl + -
	Delete selected column	Ctrl + -
	Hide a column	Ctrl + 0
	Hide a row	Ctrl + 9
	Unhide a column	Ctrl + Shift + 0
	Unhide a row	Ctrl + Shift + 9
	Group columns	Alt + Shift + Right arrow key
	Ungroup columns	Alt + Shift + Left arrow key

CHAPTER 9. PIVOT TABLES

Pivot table forms the cornerstone of the data analysis with excel. Pivot tables are the easiest way to analyze data formatted as alist.

Example Task # 26

How to insert a pivot table quickly with data in a list?

Select the data	Ctrl + Shift + down
	Ctrl + Shift + right
Access pivot table dialogue box	Alt + D + P

Example Task # 27

You want to insert a pivot chart but as a separate object. How will you do it?

To insert the pivot in new sheet	Press F1

The Keys (Used) in this Chapter

S.No	Shortcut Key	Purpose
	Open Pivot table dialogue box	Alt + D + P
	To select the pivot table	Ctrl + A
	To hide the pivot table	Ctrl + -
	To insert pivot table chart in active sheet	Alt + F1
	To insert pivot table chart in a new sheet	F1

MISCELLANEOUS

Not every user is familiar with Visual Basic for Application, the default language of MS Office. But in case you are the user of programming language, you can access the editor by pressing Alt + F11.

Example Task # 28

You arewan to access the macro dialogue box to run a macro. What is the shortcut key for it?

Access macro dialogue box	Alt + F3

The Keys (Used) in this Chapter

S.No	Shortcut Key	Purpose
	Open VBA Editor	Alt + F11
	Access the Macro dialogue box	Alt + F3
	Access spelling dialogue box	F7

WORKING WITH TOOLTIPS TO WORK FASTER

Tooltips are agreat way to access the ribbon menus of Excel. One can virtually access any feature available in the menus with these tooltips. As we have seen in the preceding chapters, most of the generic shortcuts do not relate to the ribbon menu.

In this section, we will briefly take overview of the features we can access through this option. For this option to work, you always have to start by pressing "**Alt.**"

Step 1		Step 2		Step 3
Press **Alt** Button	➔	Press **Key** for the Tab you want to access	➔	Press **Key** for the feature you want to access

Selecting the desired tab

The tab you want can be selected by just pressing the alphabet key followed by Alt Key. The following picture shows the possible options that can be used to choose the tab:

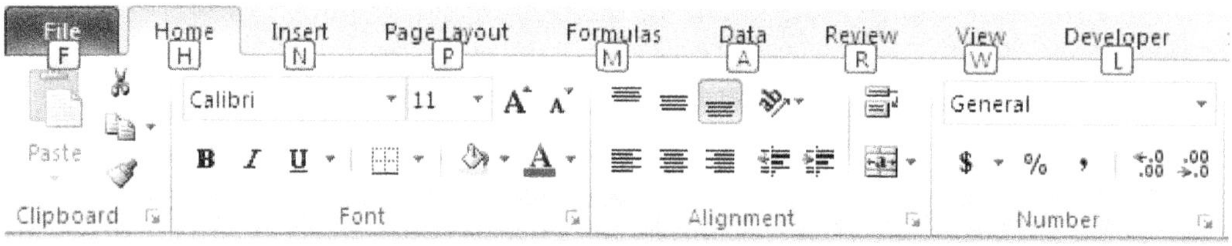

Summary of Options Available From Various Tabs

To Access		Press
To access the file menu to save file, save thefile as a new file, open and close a file.		Alt + F
To format text for font, font size, borders, copy and paste options, alignment, number formatting, conditional formatting and table options and more.		Alt + H
To insert a pivot table and chart, charts, clip art, pictures, shapes, slicers, hyperlink, textbox, header and footer, and signatures.		Alt + N
To adjust themes, margins, paper orientation, size, breaks and print area, and more.		Alt + P
To access category wise formulas and for formula auditing tools.		Alt + M
To get external data, manage data connections, tools for manipulating data like sort and filter, removing duplicates and adding data validation.		Alt + A

To Access		Press
To review the document –for example for using tools like spelling, research, thesaurus, translate function, adding acomment and for protecting aworksheet, workbook and for sharing a workbook.		Alt + R
To Adjust workbook view, to show or hide formula bar, gridlines, headings, to change zoom and windows option and to access the Macros.	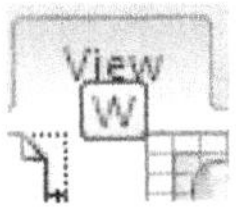	Alt + W
To access developer options like visual core, accessing recorded macros, to access add-ins, basic visual controls, and XML options.		Alt + L

Chapter 10. Tab Layout

The Home Tab

Home tab is the most used tab in Excel. There are various options available after you select the initial**Alt + H**.

Submenu Name	**Clipboard**
Access Key	Alt + H

Using clipboard menu

The clipboard contains options to paste, cut, and copy and format tool. Within clipboard submenu, you can access options using these key combinations.

Paste Options

There are two possible versions of Paste option available:

If you have copied something.

If you have not copied anything.

If you have copied	**If you have not copied**
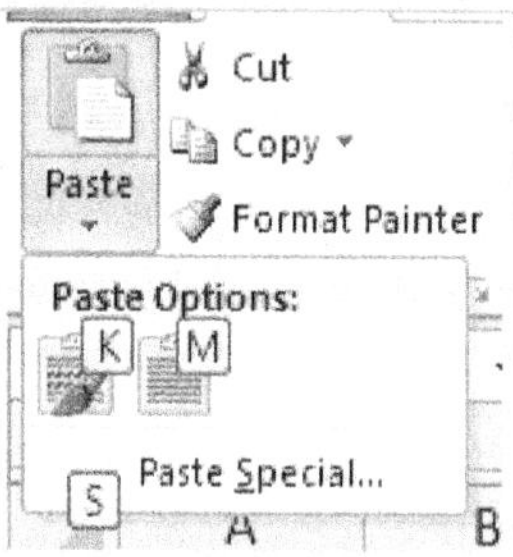	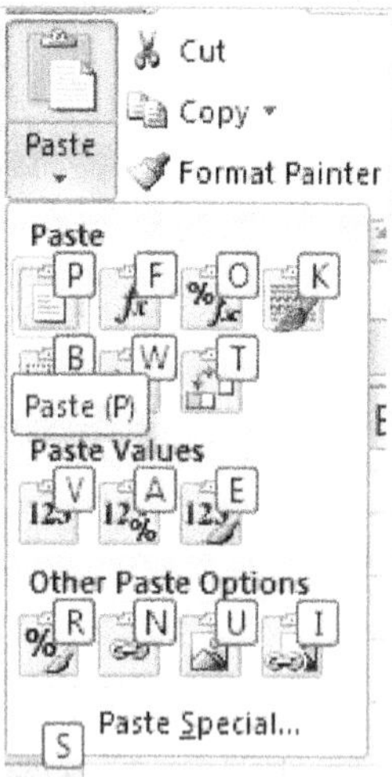

Possible Operations with Paste Shortcut Keys

Here are some possible key combinations that can be helpful when using thekeyboard:

Option	Key Combination
Paste the value as it is	Alt + H + V
Paste the value as function	Alt + H + F
Paste the value as function but keeping the original formatting	Alt + H + O
Paste but keep source formatting	Alt + H + K
Paste without any border	Alt + H + B

Paste with fixed column width	Alt + H + W
Paste Transposed	Alt + H + T
Paste Value only	Alt + H + V
Paste as link	Alt + H + N
Access the paste special Dialogue box	Alt + H + S

Cut Copy and Format Painter:

If you want to remove contents from a cell, you need to use **Cut** Option. If you want it to be on some other place as well, you can **Paste**. And if you want something to be formatted like other, you can use the **Format Painter** Option.

Following are the key combination for these three tasks.

Option	Key Combination
Cut	Alt + H + X
Copy	Alt + H + C
Paste	Alt + H + V

The Font and the Alignment Option

These set of options provide following ways to format the content:

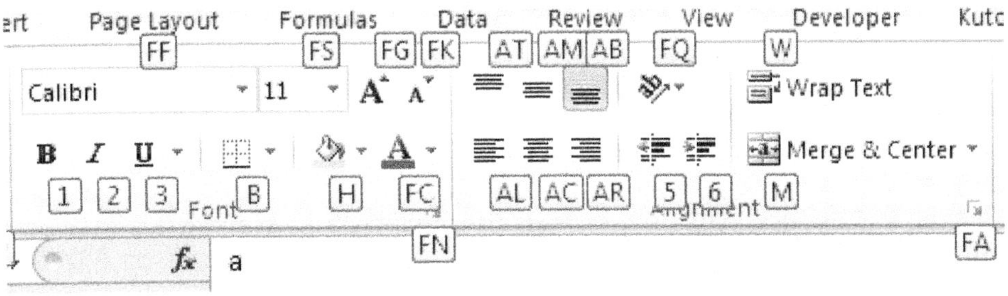

The Font Section:

You can format contents for bold, italic and underlined:

Option	Key Combination
Format Bold	Alt + H + 1
Format Italic	Alt + H + 2
Format Underlined	Alt + H + 3

The font size and type can be changed with following keys – note that key combination for accessing the **Font Options** in the **Home** Tab is **Alt + H + F** followed by options **G, K, S** and **F.**

Option	Key Combination
Grow Font	Alt + H + FG

Shrink Font	Alt + H + FK
Change Font Size by entering a value	Alt + H + FS
Change Font Type	Alt + H + FF

You can remember the above by using pegging – **G for Grow, K for Knell down, S for Size** and **F for Font**.

Alignment, Numbers and Styles Options:

To give a more professional look, the excel contents need to be aligned and sometimes indented as well. Similarly the number could be percentages, currencies or pure numbers with comma separation.

We can also use conditional formatting for formatting individual ranges as well as theuse of tables can boost productivity.

All these options are accessible through the **Home** Tab – as shown in the following picture:

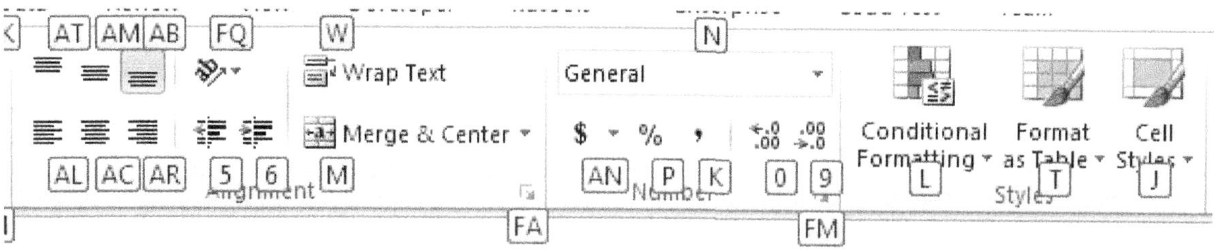

Alignment Options

Option	Key Combination
Align Top	Alt + H + AT
Align Middle	Alt + H + AM
Align Bottom	Alt + H + AB
Align Left	Alt + H + AL
Align Center	Alt + H + AC
Align Right	Alt + H + AR

We can note the pattern in the above keys – we can access the **Align Options** with **Alt + H + A** followed by characters T, M, B, L, C and R. We can remember these options like this: **T for Top, M for Middle, B for Bottom, L for left, C for center and R for Right.**

Indentation and Text Orientation Options

Option	Key Combination
Decrease Indent	Alt + H + 5
Increase Indent	Alt + H + 6
Orientation of Text	Alt + H + FQ

To reach out further options for orienting text you can choose among **O, L, U, V, D, and M**.

Number formatting Options:

The number can be formatted as a number, as apercentage, as currency or can be written in scientific mode. The following three are most used options in number submenu.

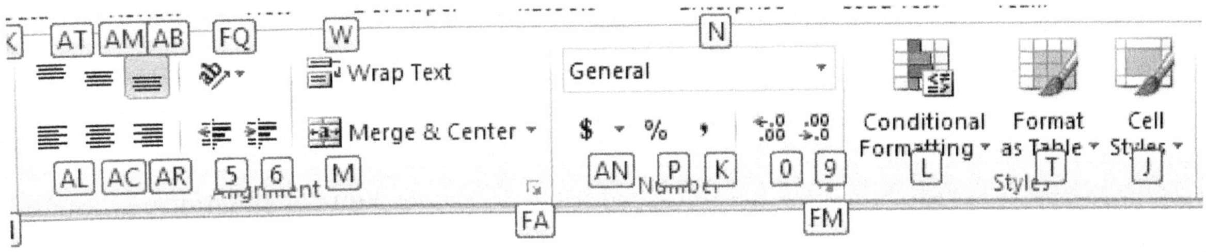

Number formatting Options

Option	Key Combination
Format as in accounting	Alt + H + AN
Format as currency	Alt + H +P
Format as Date	Alt + H + K
For increasing significant number	Alt + H + 0
For decreasing significant numbers	Alt + H + 9

Styles, Cell and Editing Options

In this part we can use conditional formatting to format cells when they meet the set criteria, we can insert and delete cells and format them. We have also opted to sort and filter data, to find something and various other options.

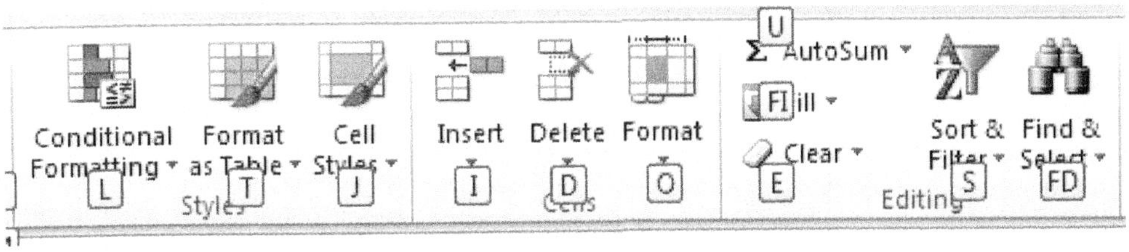

Number formatting Options

Option	Key Combination
Use conditional formatting menu	Alt + H + L
Format a range of cells as table	Alt + H +T
Access cell styles menu	Alt + H + J
Insert Cells	Alt + H + I

Delete Cells	Alt + H + D
Format Cells	Alt + H + O

Here **D is for Delete, I for Insert, T for table.**

Editing Options

Option	Key Combination
Auto-sum cells	Alt + H +U
Fill Out a Pattern	Alt + H + F
Sort and filter	Alt + H + S

The Insert Tab

Through the insert menu we can insertany thing ranging from a pivot table to a chart and an object like picture or a hyperlink.

The Tables, Illustrations and Chart Options:

Following are the shortcut keys to most frequent used shortcut keys:

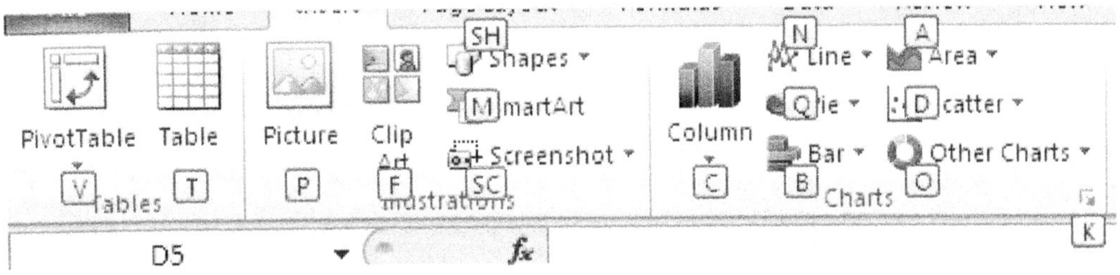

Tables and Illustration Options

Option	Key Combination
Inserting a Pivot Table	Alt + N + V
Inserting a Picture	Alt + N + P
Insert a Clipart	Alt + N + F
Insert a Screenshot	Alt + N + SC
Insert a Shape	Alt + N +SH
Insert Smart Art	Alt + N + M

The pattern in the above shortcut keys should be noted and is easy to remember – **P for Picture, SC for thescreenshot, SH for Shape and M for Smart.** In this way, you can remember the keys.

Chart Options

Option	Key Combination
Insert a column chart	Alt + N + C
Insert a Bar chart	Alt + N + B
Insert a Line chart	Alt + N + N
Insert area chart	Alt + N + A
Insert a Pie chart	Alt + N + Q
Insert any other chart	Alt + N + O

Again we can remember the keys using these connections – **C for Column, B for Bar, N for Line, A for Area, and O for other charts.**

The Sparkline, Filter, Text, and Symbols:

The sparklines are very useful in-cell charts. In excel 2010 they have been introduced as a built-in feature in excel. Filter section includes anoption to insert a slicer but for excel 2010 slicers only works with apivot table. We can insert text items like header and footer, word art and signature line as well as equation and symbols from this part.

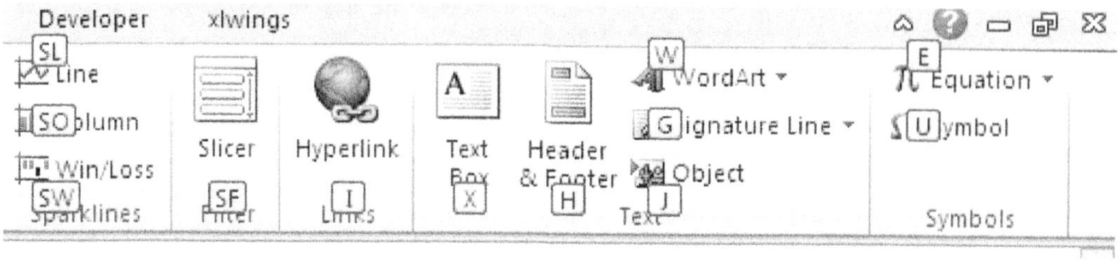

Sparkline, Slicers and Hyperlink Options

Option	Key Combination
Line type Sparkline	Alt + N + SL
Column type Sparkline	Alt + N + SO
Win-Loss Sparkline	Alt + N + W
Insert a Slicer	Alt + N + SF
Insert a Hyperlink	Alt + N + I

Remembering Sparkline keys are easy – **L for Line Type, O for Column type, W for Win-Loss. SF for Slicer Filter and I for Hyperlink.**

THE PAGE LAYOUT TAB

This tab houses all the options that are related to pay layout – themes, colors, fonts and effects, margins, orientation, breaks, etc. We will take up one by one this subsection and will see how we can be more productive with shortcut keys.

The Sparkline, Filter, Text, and Symbols:

Theme Options

The general key to access the theme options is to use Alt + N + T followed by desired option key.

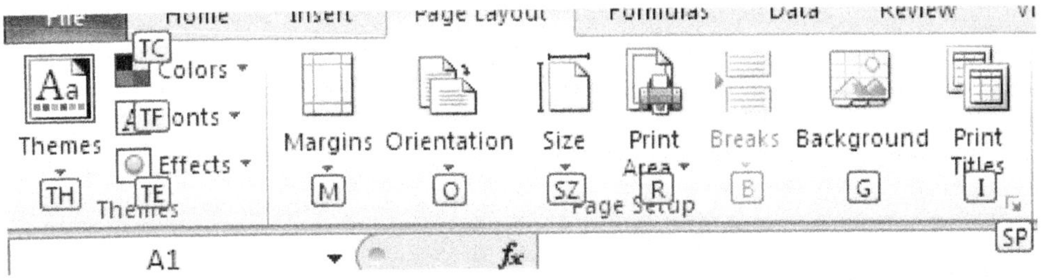

Option	Key Combination
Access themes	Alt + N + T H
Access Colors	Alt + N + T C
Access Fonts	Alt + N + T F
Access Effects	Alt + N + T E

In above shortcut keys, **C represents Color, F for fonts and E for effects.**

Page Layout Options

Option	Key Combination
Setting up Margins	Alt + N + M
Orientation setup	Alt + N + O
Page Size	Alt + N + S Z
Breaks	Alt + N + B
Background	Alt + N + G
Printing Titles	Alt + N + I
Scale to Fit	Alt + N + X

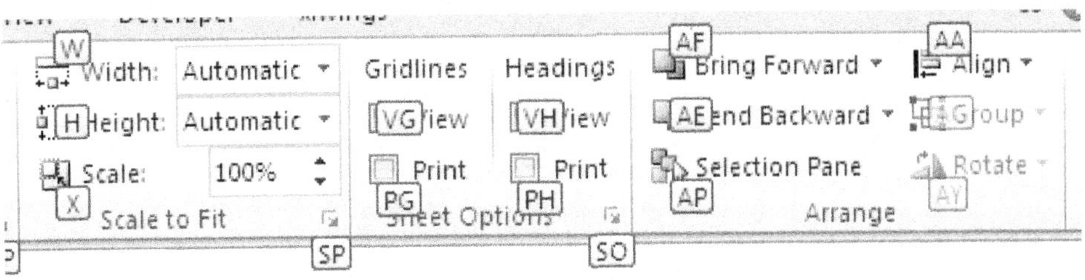

You can remember these keys this way: **M for Margins, O for Orientation, SZ for size, B for breaks, G for Background.**

THE FORMULA TAB

The usual shortcut key to access the formula dialogue box Is **Shift + F3**, but if you want to access the formula using Formula tab, you should press **Alt + M** that should give you access to different of functions as well as to formula validation options.

These are the shortcut keys to access the different types of function in this tab:

Function Options

Option	Key Combination
Insert a function	Alt + M + A
Recently used functions	Alt + M + R
Logical functions	Alt + M + L
Text functions	Alt + M + T
Math and Trigonometric functions	Alt + M + G
Financial functions	Alt + M + I
Date and time functions	Alt + M + E
More functions	Alt + M + Q

Some of the shortcuts are easy identifiable how they are created for example **R for Recently used function, L for logical, T for text function**. Others can be remembered with a little bit of difficulty like **G for math and trigonometric function, I for Financial functions, E for date and time functions.**

Defined Names and Formula auditing Options:

When a cell is frequently used or if the methods are complicated, it is easier to refer to a cell with a name then a cell address. A cell name also makes formulas more meaningful and less prone to errors.

With formula auditing toolbar, we can check the input and out of a formula for errors and find if there is one in it or not.

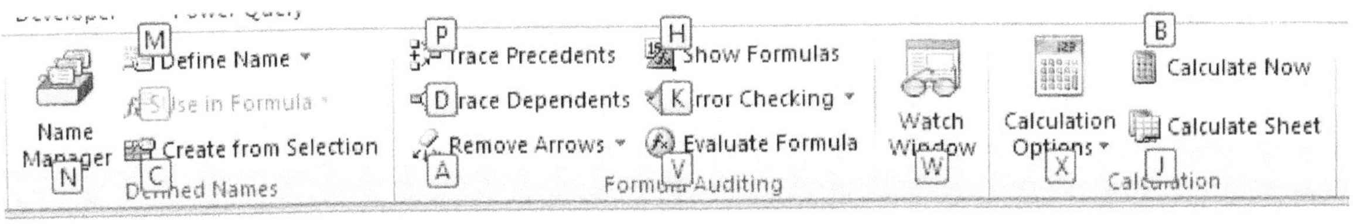

Following are the shortcut keys for these two options.

Named range and formula auditing Options

Option	Key Combination

Option	Key Combination
Accessing Name Manager Dialogue Box	Alt + M + N
Define Name	Alt + M + M
Create Name from Selection	Alt + M + C
Trace Precedents	Alt + M + P
Trace Dependents	Alt + M + D
Show Formulas	Alt + M + H
Check Errors	Alt + M + K
Evaluate Formulas	Alt + M + V
Access Calculation Options	Alt + M + X

For this table, **N is for Name Manager, C is to create aname from selection, P for tracing precedents, D is for dependents** and so on.

The Data Tab

The data tab houses options to suffice the requirement related to database management. It allows you to manipulate data, import data and sort and filter it. You can bring in data from applications like access, from web, for text file (.txt) and from few other sources.

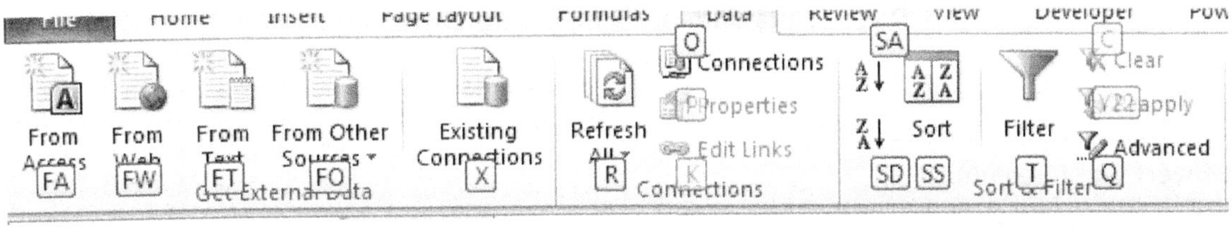

Besides this you can filter and sort your data, and you can use advanced filter options.

Get External Data, Connection and Sort and Filter Options

Option	Key Combination
Getting Data from MS Access	Alt + A + F A
Getting Data from Web	Alt + A + F W
Getting Data from Text File	Alt + A + F T
Getting Data from other sources	Alt + A + F O
To check existing connections	Alt + A + X
To Refresh connections	Alt + A + R
Sort Ascending	Alt + A + S A
Sort Descending	Alt + A + S D
Filter Data	Alt + A + F
Advanced Filter	Alt + A + Q

The essential key to access the data source options is **Alt + M + A + F** followed by **Aif you want it from Access, W if you want it from Web, T if from atext file and O if from Other sources.**

Data Tools and Outlining Data Options:

Data tools are used to transform data for example by converting text to column based on delimiter value or by removing duplicates or grouping and ungrouping data.

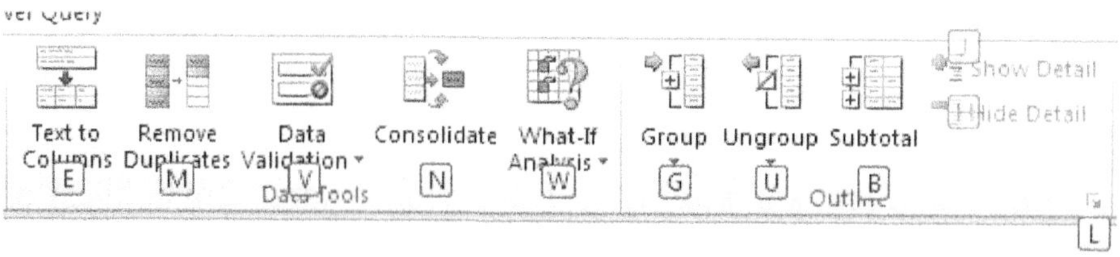

Data Tools and Outlining Data Options

Option	Key Combination
To convert text to column	Alt + A + E
To remove duplicates	Alt + A + M
To apply data validation	Alt + A + V
Perform what-if analysis	Alt + A + W
Group data	Alt + A + G
Ungroup data	Alt + A + U
Add subtotal	Alt + A + B

In above shortcuts, **V can be remembered for Validation, W for What if analysis, G for grouping, U for ungrouping and B for Subtotal.**

THE REVIEW TAB

The review tab helps you correct spellings, do research and check athesaurus, translate and add comments to the file. It allows you to protect the worksheet and workbooks and to share it with your colleagues.

Following is the screenshot of the tab, once you have selected the options**Alt + R** where **R stands for Review.**

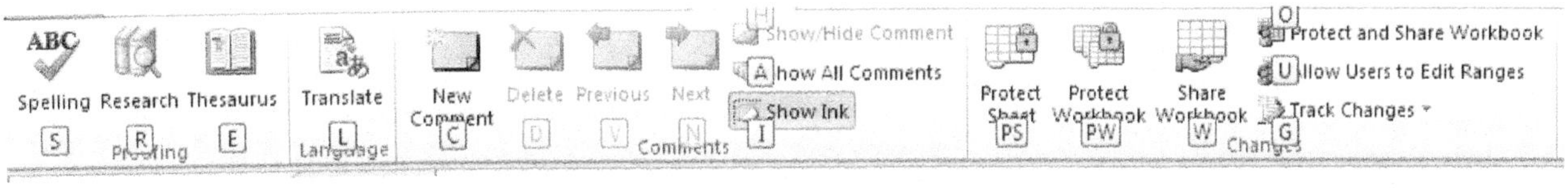

Review Tab Options

Option	Key Combination
Check for spelling	Alt + R + S
Use thesaurus	Alt + R + E
Translate	Alt + R + L
Add a new comments	Alt + R + C
Show all comments	Alt + R + A
Protect sheet	Alt + R + PS
Protect Workbook	Alt + R + PW
Share Workbook	Alt + R + W
Protect and Share	Alt + R + O
Allow users to edit ranges	Alt + R + U
Track Changes	Alt + R + G

THE VIEW TAB

This tab is meant to adjust the view of theworksheet. It allows us to set workbook view, show or hide gridlines, headings, ruler and formula bar, to set zoom value, to arrange how the windows are arranged and more.

The workbook view, show, and zoom options:

The workbook can be viewed in either normal mode, in page layout mode or page break preview mode. Following are the shortcut keys we used for this part:

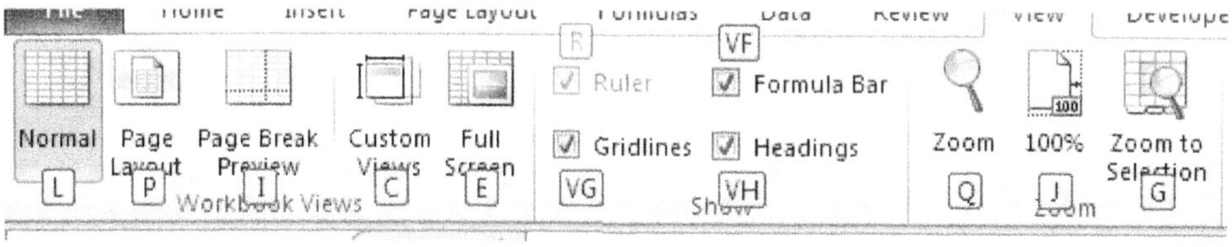

The workbook view, show and zoom options

Option	Key Combination
View in normal mode	Alt + W + L
View in Page layout mode	Alt + W + P
View in Page break mode	Alt + W + I
Setup a custom view	Alt + W + C
Setup a full screen view	Alt + W + E

Here **P is for page layout mode, C can be remembered for custom views mode**.

Windows Options and Macros

When you are working with more than one excel files, these options comes in handy. You can arrange worksheets to you ease and freeze pans so that header does not go anywhere. Following are the options that are available at your disposal.

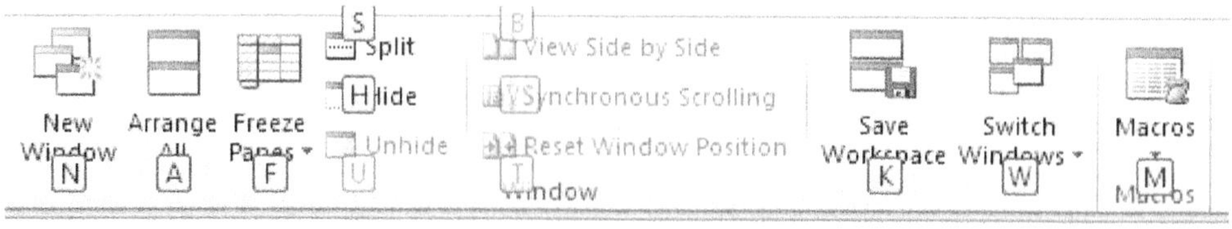

Option	Key Combination
Open workbook in a new window	Alt + W + N
Arrange windows	Alt + W + A
Freeze Panes	Alt + W + F
Split windows	Alt + W + S
Hide windows	Alt + W + H

Option	Key Combination
Save a workplace	Alt + W + K
Switch Windows	Alt + W + W
Access Macros	Alt + W + M

CHAPTER 11. CREATING YOUR SHORTCUTS

How many times you have to the point when you are unable to find the shortcut key for an operation. It is often cased that the exhaustive shortcut key list misses that one single shortcut key that we need to improve the productivity to get through a repetitive task.

With Excel's Key Tips are sufficient to access any key if that is not found in the shortcut keys list, we can still be more productive by *recording macros and assigning keys to them to perform the repetitive tasks.*

So in this part of the book, we will show you how to handle such custom requirement and be more productive!

Example # 01

Filling selection with a custom fill

We can follow the Key Tips to access the color fill menu. Just press Alt + H + H and select the color of your choice towant to fill by using arrow keys. But to perform a more accurateoption, you have to use various options. For example in the following picture, we need to use several options to get the result.

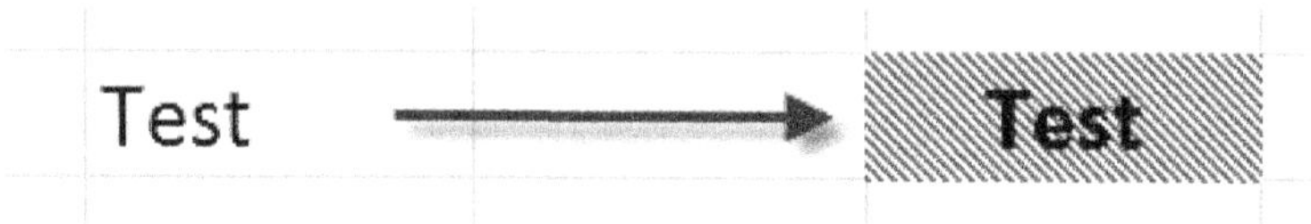

Here the solution is to record a macro and edit it for what we need. Here is the edited code when we record the macro.

```
Sub MyFormatTextMacro()
    With Selection
        .Font.ColorIndex = xlAutomatic
        .Interior.Pattern = xlDown
        .Interior.PatternColor = 255
        .Interior.ColorIndex = xlAutomatic
        .Font.Bold = True
        .HorizontalAlignment = xlCenter
        .VerticalAlignment = xlCenter
    End With
End Sub
```

Now once it has been recorded, we can assign it a shortcut key so that when we press keys, the macrorun.

Example # 02

We have shortcut keys for copying data from Top and Right side of the cells, but what if we want to copy from the left end of a cell. This is unusual as most of the time we move from top to bottom and from left to right though.

Let's see how can we set keys for this littleshortcut.

```
Sub copyfromleft()
ActiveCell = ActiveCell.Offset(0, 1)
End Sub
```

Assigning this macro a shortcut key will enable us to copy from the right side of the cell as well.

Example # 03

Let's take one more example of setting up a shortcut key for copying cells formula. The active is currently displaying the value or result of a formula, but you are interested in the unevaluated formula expression that should be copied by the side of that cell. Ideally, it should look like:

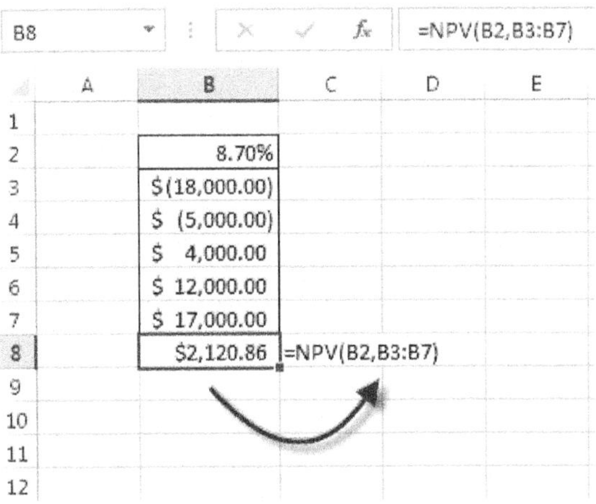

The following macro achieves the task and if shortcut keys are assigned to it, will work like charm:

```
Sub CopyFormulaToLeft()
If ActiveCell.HasFormula Then ActiveCell.Offset(0, 1) = "'"
&CStr(ActiveCell.Formula)
End Sub
```

Thus you can create shortcuts of your own with small VBA codes to automate tasks.

CPSIA information can be obtained
at www.ICGtesting.com
Printed in the USA
BVOW08s1721220418
513937BV00007B/359/P

9 781948 433082